Charismatic Megafauna

Tamsin Kendrick studied Philosophy and Theology at Oxford University before launching herself into London's vibrant performance poetry scene. Since then she has appeared at literary festivals and venues all over the world, including mini-tours of Ireland and New York. Her poetry has been published in *The Delinquent, The Wolf, The Fix, Tears in the Fence* and *Rising*. She works as a freelance writer and editor in South London.

Charismatic Megafauna

Tamsin Kendrick

penned in the margins

PUBLISHED BY PENNED IN THE MARGINS
53 Arcadia Court, 45 Old Castle Street, London E1 7NY
www.pennedinthemargins.co.uk

First published 2009

Printed in the United Kingdom by MPG Biddles Ltd.

ISBN
0-9553846-5-6
978-0-9553846-5-3

Contents

I

II

III

ACKNOWLEDGEMENTS

Acknowledgements are due to the editors/producers of *The Delinquent*, *The Fix*, *The Wolf*, *Rising*, *Tears in the Fence*, *Poetcasting*, *Tears in the Fence*, Parlour Games (Resonance FM) and The Verb (BBC Radio 3).

~

Thanks to all the poets in my life who never knew when to go home, and to my parents who made my home a wonderful place to be.

Charismatic Megafauna

So that no corner can hide you, no autumn of leaves
So deeply close over you that I shall not find you,
To stretch down my hand and sting you with life
Like poison that resurrects.
>   George Barker, 'O Who will speak from a Womb or a
>   Cloud?'

Sometimes she became so lost in thought, she could not see where she was
walking. At other times, it seemed as if she acted without any thought at
all and had to spend her wakeful hours making up stories about why she
did things.
>   Greg Keyes, *The Black God*

I

Proverbs I

If this was a story, a sword
would be pulled from a stone,
a magic ring flung
into the depths of the sea
and with general rejoicing
the world would turn

and I would no longer be the girl
sitting in your run-down flat

waiting for you to look at me.

Lancing

The bird quivers cup-sized in his Montana palms.

The physician does what the poet cannot,
scalpels the rotten interior,
knight-lances the troubling,
buckling glands that knot a throat-neck,
moulding broke-back with steadying hands.

I am the swans spying the penthouse shadows,
gliding the tide beneath the balcony.
I crane the angle of my alabaster grace
to where you pad, love-striped before the fire,
tiger-eyed, cornfield-armed. I'm charmed

as you purify a needle kiss with a candle flame,
anaesthetise me with wine and stillness,
operate on my soreness. Afterwards
cartooning the tips of me blush pink with Disney plasters.

If I could I'd buy back your grandfather's piano,
pawned long ago to a suburban warehouse,
so I can hear you play Rachmaninoff again,
so I would own the notes beneath your fingers.

Charismatic Megafauna

I have travelled far in Japanese silk slippers;
the geishas broke my feet. I wear a fedora hat
for mystery solving and brandy drinking,
a rag tag of skirts, leggings, a naked knee,
a burn on my thigh, a blood dream.

Towards the Temple I open.

Gold rings on three of my fingers, for bartering,
for proof I am the child of the electric priest
and his red-headed Jew, full of breast,
whom he loved and rescued from the suburbs

but refused to sing to. Introverted,

he paces the roof garden and mumbles
strange languages beneath a sky that loves him.
His footsteps pop with new life. The trees harmonise.

This is where I began, nestled small in the pelvis
of an acoustic. Chords vibrating bones,
pickings trembling skin. Daddy is music

floating through the bedroom ceiling, Daddy is love,
incense, promises tied to red bows. Daddy is my passage

through the avenue of vines, the gatekeeper to the synagogue.
He holds my hand as towards the Temple we open.

Beecow

If I could be anything for you
I'd be a cross between a bee and a cow.
I'd succour you with milk and honey,
sweeten your lips and cover you with cream.
But with a sting the size of an udder
you'd be too frightened to make the wrong move.

Mooing between buzzes I'd sound ridiculous,
be cow clumsy and hefty in flight.
But I wouldn't mind: if you laughed at me
I'd squash you flat like a grand piano
crash-landing on Broadway.

Peter Pan Versus Captain Hook

My friend vouched a theory that all men were either
Peter Pans or Captain Hooks. I don't know about you but

I know where I stand. Look what that bastard did to poor Wendy;
Tinkerbell too. I'll have no truck with flighty boys.

Give me instead the feel of steel on my thigh,
the screams of pirates trapped in the boo-boo box.

But most of all give me the whispery hair under the wig,
the gnarled hand, the hook trailing red lines down my abdomen.

He pulls my hair, holds his hook to *my* mouth, then, suddenly shy,
his mouth. No thimbles in sight. Finally, a real kiss.

Loveland, Colorado

As they hurtled through Loveland,
past the lake and the school, she
wondered what exactly she expected.

The answer couldn't be simple;
that wouldn't be enough.
She needed rescuing, paying, loving.
She needed to do a damn good job.

Later, as the rocks blazed a brilliant red
through the panorama of her window,
she suddenly had this thought.
What if this was the beginning

of something promised?
What if here and now, God stretched down
two fingers and stung her with life.
Like lightning that resurrects.

Bear Lake, Colorado

For Kay

We fought the weather to reach Bear Lake,
slipping down snowdrifts, stomping
in twin white coats, trainers, slithering and
giggling as other walkers passed, wondering

at our lack of snow shoes, ski-jackets,
preparation. We arrived at a clearing that
you assured me was water. Beneath
the snow, the shore and lake were

impossible to tell apart. I walked on the ice,
joking, "I'm Jesus!" Who cares if it's cheating.

I have a photo. There is evidence this time.

Dating Criteria

I mainly started dating him
so I'd have someone to

watch my stuff when I
went to the bathroom.

He had his good points.
He never stole anything

or spiked my drink
with Rohypnol or MDMA.

For my part
I never spent too long on

the loo (I pee quickly)
and always laughed at his jokes.

There's a lot to be said
for people who take care

of things in your absence.
For those who protect

what is yours.

Of Mice and Men

Butterfly knickers bare to French doors
that open to the garden. He carries her down
the stairs. The sunlight silhouettes her thighs
through the Paisley skirt. She was young

back then, but he was young too.
Protests first, but she soon sank
to it; you see she'd planned it, excited
as her mother dropped her by the train.

Her love for him was like that half-wit
brother, shot in the forest by what he loved.
Better to kill it quick before the world
does it for you; better to shoot it in the

head before the congregation gets there,
their flaming torches, their golden eyes.
It was summer; French doors open
to the garden, her legs prey legs,

all sinew and knee, buckling. He starts to lick.
At seventeen he was the oldest man she'd ever.

South Bank Beach

We perch on salty stone
freckled with mud and birdshit,
facing the flow as it taunts
us with *spirillum* minus and currents

that can strip a corpse down to an
American size zero in the time it
took Christ to resurrect.
There's no driftwood or conch shells;

just Tesco jellyfish and Evian shoals.
On the surface, tangles of fishbone
and scum foam like the brown
bubbles on crème brûlée.

In your arms the usual clockwork
of my flesh smelts to Dali melts,
the wind and wine a chemical peel
on my cheeks. We hang our

heads over the side, stretch
our lovebitten necks towards
the water. The bends crush
our windpipes. You curve my arms

to tango, dangle me over the staircase.
I shriek, delighted at the danger of it all.
No. Wait. It's not that,
it's the strength of your arms.

My heady freedom.
The sheer fucking beauty of us.

An Irish Dream

For Neil McCarthy

Horror as I struggled through shifting
landscapes: Kurtz's bloody jungle,
Virginia's waves, Mickey Mouse

axing Goofy in cartoon suburbia.
The pills had gone deep this time,
chasing a lost phone, a funfair ride.

You appeared at the door, fingers dipped
in all those countries of yours, France, Spain;
blurring the air around you with kindness.

You call my name. My throat opens in a raw scream,
wet with phlegm and the entropy of sleep;
startling the housekeeper in the hallway.

You vow never to bring me tea in bed again.

Bloody Mare

She's coming over charcoal seas, sliding with kelp and weed,
Franz Marc's mare, electric with London's red neon,
plunge-diving, bunching and smoothing into gallop,
cantering up the Corrib into Galway.

Skittering on the bank, she scatters swans,
sweat foaming on her flanks, saliva from bit,
escaped from paddock, hustling for oats,
barley. She's used to class, upkeep.

The physician moves closer, brandishing fire.
This is her life, this branding; at least make the wound deep.
She's got little time to spare. Suddenly petrified eyes
condense, sharpen. What concrete angel will

she call for now? One with a saddle, a pair of reigns?
One with a blanket, a gypsy's heart to steer her away?
The wildness she was given in the womb as foal
won't depart, won't shift an electron, a spark.

How can she be broken in, whipped to victory?
By whom and to where, she knows neither.

If there are green pastures, lay her down.
If there is more than this, give her the gift
or take the shotgun from the outhouse wall,

cock the barrel, finish this.

Into the Woods

My most post-modern Mr Tumnus,
mushroom pale and autumn haired,
you pop me a wink and flex your spring-bones,
produce a lute and start to sing.

We go deep into the woods.
The birds watch our happening,
orchestrate our pathway,
jewel and pearl the cedar trees, full throated.

I am lake-born, filled with green water,
flashes of rainbow scales, depths and
fairy tales, a thousand sunk crowns; the circles
of your swimming swell the whole of me.

You corner me for a drink.
Inside you discover fish heads and bracken,
a snapping pike, a flash of gold.
Iridescent shoals nibble at your fingers.

You dip into me and dip out;
this unleaning churns me to wave.
I keel towards you and keen,
but I will not kneel. Not yet.

I pool myself on your broad shoulders,
dribble on your clavicle. The poplar trees hiss.
You laugh with them, tear off my shoes,
dance deeper into the woods, kiss an ankle,

bite a shin, slip a hand over the ebb of me,
pour me into your clearing,
next to your shack and smoker,
settle me into your shores.

The leaves drift onto my surface,
the blossom too. I call to you:

Come swimming, my love; dive deep.
Swim down and pick out a crown.
Swim strong and brave and bold;
I promise I won't let you drown.

Mr Tumnus Comes to London

I watched your white eyebrows wriggling,
neon glowworms beside the breakfast table.
Too big for your chair, you slouched feral
and unwashed, stained feet caressing

the laminate. I remembered your hunger,
made salmon and hen eggs, butternut soup,
apple crumble. I wore an apron and flicked my hair,
pretended not to notice as you choked mouthfuls down.

The night before we spun riddles and word games
into thick vacant air. I won every one.
You held me over the cushions.
And I was proud of myself.

When the trains thudded outside the window
you winced and made me ashamed of my home.
I lied and told you they stopped at night.
I thought if I could hold you hard enough

I'd deafen you.

In the early hours my sister returned home.
She whispered on the stairs, "Is everything okay?"
I held her arm and mouthed, "Yes".

In the morning, in the middle of it,
I sent you out for cigarettes, so I'd have something
to do whilst I watched you finish it.
As you explained, you began to cry.

I trailed smoke off the balcony and watched
you curiously. You cried some more so I told you to leave.
Embarrassed, I called my mother and told her she was
never going to get to meet you.

I smoked my cigarettes and tried to pray,
remembered all the things you had given me:
a cup of salty tea, a dress, a scalpel wound,
three bite marks and a couple of beers.

All in all, I think you'll agree.
You came off far better than me.

I Dream of Tumnus

I have no red cloak, nor know the way.
The trees tangle my hair with shadows.
I do not sing. I can't. The wind frightens me.

The woodcutters ignore me. I've lost my basket,
my shoes; my snagged feet bleed on dead leaves.

Yesterday I found the village girl's abortion,
fretting and mewing beneath the poplar trees.
He died as I held him;
touch, it seemed, was the last straw.

If I was more than this I'd build a tree-house,
catch a hare, make a stew with wild roots;
bathe in streams, make faces at the badgers.
Instead I am motionless. Slugs and snails

make silvery trails over my thighs.
Spiders web my hair with dew.
Woodlice curl in my ears.
Time passes and I am bracken.

I sink into the forest floor, camouflaged,
melting into the scenery. Waiting.

II

Proverbs II

I asked, "Why do waves have points?
Is it because they want to fly?"
You answered, "No, they've got to be that
shape so's to fit into the sky."

Tiny Dancer Does New York

We shot pool til half past four
with toothless hicks,
short drinks, silhouettes
in the shade of the haze of the room.
Background goes,
blue jean baby, LA lady.

But I'm sick,
I want Blighty,
I want a straddle hip and a dummy stick,
some soap gum and a bleach itch,
I want to be clean again.
Lay me down in sheets of linen.

I didn't ask him to sink my eight
despite what the other one said
with his eyes. Later his foot snuck up the stair
of the floor of the house to my room,

pleading in his quavering voice,
you didn't leave enough reds on the table,
you forgot not to smile.

I'm just the chalk for the end of your cue;
I'm just the girl at the end of your hall,
cheater, father, pool player.

Jesus freaks out on the street.

Ode to Blues & Gin

Gin always makes me go a little stir crazy.
It affects my best friend Liz just the same;
sometimes we cry but mostly we just get this feeling,
wanting the spinning city to lead us both astray.

I could do anything in this mood;
I could kiss a thousand boys and still have room.
I am in the Blues Bar and living up my bohemian dream;
I'm on a table and I'm dancing,
side-stepping and prancing,
knock-kneed but elastic under the light fantastic.

I may have no soul, but I have gin.
And it is wetter than and more than
and better than any wind or breath-womb,
soul-Tsunami or spirit-monsoon
you could contest me with.

I am laid down deep under the guitar, the base beat
and I am trip-hopping and lip-locking,
shockingly docking my ship-shape slim curves
into any open crotch.

I think I may have a small problem with alcohol.
For the past fifty-five days I have been sober for two;
in fact I'm writing this drunk,
hunched down and shrunk, hands shaking,
pouring another sacred other glass of gin;

you see,

gin is the scissors that cuts my imagination
from the baseline of my thought
and beautifully spiralled I am left to curve
off beyond the body that betrayed me;

the body that I sent into the world
to be among other bodies
so it could make amends,
but it just made me another G&T.

It's a skin-stitched Judas that deserves to die,

but in the meantime, as justice is dealt out
by alien hands beyond me
and angels move close behind me to catch me
and something veiled moves before me,
I'll remain ginned-up and world-hazy,
dancing in the Blues Bar, just a little stir-crazy.

This City Needs a Hero

This city needs a hero, a pathfinder;
an old school, swagger-stepped,
nimble-legged man-boy or boy-man,
or whatever you are when youth
rages like a cyclone in your loins
and playground taunts are as
fresh in your memory as the last
Tory government;

but he's not young enough to still believe in war
and he's not young enough to still believe that inside
Everyman there's a good, good man trying to blindside
the Outman with his moral charms. No. He knows
that inside Everyman there's just a snivelling little child
clawing its way through the bone.

He thinks not in straight lines but in giant amber spheres.
He's got a ram rod spine and only fears the death of the city,
the rising dark of its inhabitants.

He side-steps through the curvature of industrial geometry,
the ligature of concrete suffering that backdrops, that old lie,
that it is good and noble to get what you can get
and in getting, forgetting
what you had to do to get there in the first place.

Yeah, block the ears and wash the hands;
keep the name of God, but not his face
and never ever read the statistics
in the Sunday morning papers.

This city needs a hero, a pathfinder;
someone who is capable of finding paths
in the pathless wilderness;
who will shrink from no danger or hardship,
crack den or bar fight,
happy slapper or gang bandanna.

On Sundays, he likes to prostrate himself outside Parliament
and shake. Pin up Venn diagrams of new trade laws on the gate.
Some say the whales in the Thames came because of him,
negotiated dim waterways, embraced death, for a glance, a glance.

He writes strange words on the condensation of train windows,
prances through Soho shadows, tells eccentric stories to strangers
in bars, compares scars with boxers and boucers
(he's got quite a collection), shows affection to crack whores,
the homeless, the addicts, the tragics.
He's got the kind of magic we need.

This city needs a hero, a pathfinder,
a locust-fed manna-bringer,
a honey-dripping psalm-singer,
a street savvy, Thames navvy,
golden boy, Special K,
God of men, prince of princes, hero of heroes.

He understands when it all gets too much
and he makes it better with just one touch.

Another night in, another strange sound

The girl scratches at her pores,
digging up hesitation with
red crescent finger nails.

She prays at the altar of noise.
She has a second voice box.
The kind that croaks from the throat
of a calcified foetus. Small and perverse.

It goes, baby coo, baby boo. Guttural sounds.
It's a lie in a tin cup mouth,
tapping the tooth with the buzz, buzz,
wasp buzz of untruth.

Yesterday. For him. She morphed into a neon sign.
But proximity turned him illiterate.
She was back-lit and stencilled
against the thick musk of the room.

Squared out like a cubed crucifixion,
as wrong as reversed threes,
as wrong as his eyes so glazed he looked blind,

brain blotted drunk, mind in the sewer,
bent her fingers backwards till it screamed.
Yeah she screamed. Screeched like a kicked cat,
a napalmed child.

Spolit and kicking against his bible-gloved punch.
Right in the plasma pumper,

left breast wobbling a little as it whacked through.

Thinking all the time, *I hope it leaves a bruise,*
God, I hope it leaves a bruise.
Then I'll have something to show, to own,
to put in little boxes and use.

Curve

The one before carved me.
This one does not carve. He curves instead,
curves me like he curves the air with chords.
So I crave him, curl like a chordshape,
crouch, a B7 in his fingers' care.

Windmill

We met
at another one of those endless
poetry nights,

the ones
where everyone seems to
turn up.

I felt faint
so you offered me a wall
to lean on.

I liked
your kindness and your height,
your curly hair.

Around me
the place was packed. Strange:
we were all there.

The usual suspects.
Much later you told me your family
owned a windmill.

At that moment
you had me in the palm of your hand.

Close your eyes now.

Turn over.

Western Front

Out! Out! Quick, girls! An ecstasy of dancing,
balancing on red wine heels, corkscrew eyes,
the ladies negotiate their fronts through the West side

of London.

Marching down from Crystal Palace, racing together
over city streets on two-inch Topshop studded leathers, knickers
exposed, and instantly the whole town burns
for their blood and drink after drink
offered in exchange for their lips; and the sweaty club walls
boom and flex, spiral away to drug-addled depths.

It's the end of the night; they're knock-kneed, bent like beggars,
vomiting in ditches, cursing through London sludge,
phlegm gargling from Marlboro-corrupted lungs.
Some have lost their shoes, but trudge on, blind drunk,
deaf to the early morning hoots of tired, half-stripped

lads from Manchester.

My friend, if you could see them tripping down
toilet stairs, landing on cars, breasts unleashed
and quivering on twilight bars.

You would not sing with desperate glory that old lie,
with groping glee:

don't you wish your girlfriend was hot like me?

Seaside & Chips

The unfamiliar hit us in the face on a Saturday afternoon by the seaside. You fed me chips as I forced my eyes to the place where the grey sea met the grey sky in a blur of incertitude & I thought, once, back then when the world was much bigger, someone with ridiculous mathematical exactness named it *horizon* & was smug and happy with themselves for a while & we were stuck with a name too neat for its imprecision & we wondered what other words we were no longer able to use.

Then in tandem we stared down at our shoes, at the rising tide before us, its lapping wetness, a monstrous dog snuffling at our trainers, then five metres further out at the blue-black heads that kept waving about their shock white hair & head banging down, down to the ocean floor.

And I thought

Why does the ocean hurt so much that it breaks at our feet, on our shores & why does the earth creak & groan at our doors & the mountains tumble down to us, falling rocks like falling stone tears, & the ground shakes so much it tears & the breaking of the head of the waves doesn't stop & soon they become large white arms balancing on the tips of waves begging to be dragged tsunami shaped past the beachhead & into the land beyond

& by my side my fingers flex to try to spread net wide to catch the catch & my heart thuds in empathy, boo-boom, rush, boo-boom, rush & my thoughts bubble up foam white & churning, as the sky kaleidoscopes in on itself & everything's turning

& yes, of course, every wave has power somewhere within me & they wriggle like fishes & make me giggle sometimes & I start to laugh

& you & you ask if I want another chip & the sea-spell is broken & I don't know if you were thinking the same thing, but if you were you would have added sea-kittens for decoration & a primary yellow sun in the corner, it's why I like you so much, you give me other people's thoughts.

Faults on the Line

Mermaid my ankles with gold wire;
use a cross stitch and a knitting needle.

Coat my hair in scarlet wax;
use a candelabra and a blowtorch.

Tattoo my skin blue;
use ladybug blood and a sharpened ball point.

Lay me face down on the railway line;
use tenderness and two palms.

Nail an express train to my tailbone;
use a silver chain and a jackhammer.

Secure it tight. Stoke the fire.
Show me the right track.

You Kiss Hard, Like I Do

Hail was no less strong than your mouth,
hard like the acorn you once drew
to explain the growth of small things.

(If I read it right, the cartoon in the book
was a palm reading, a Christian tarot?)

I wanted you to draw me, capture me; explain.
This is my gift back. Explaining nothing.

2040AD

We Are What We Are

The war continues. We forget why.
The internet shows soldiers vomiting in deserts.
After the power stations are bombed
there is no more news.

Aeroplanes disappear, turn up
days later as oil slicks on beaches.
Rationing begins, the bread queues
riot, a child is killed, the crowds

storm Parliament. Polio returns
with the rats, as does the pox,
mumps and rabies, then something
worse. Technology dies with the scientists.

Winters dance with electric storms.
We barter wedding rings for aspirin.
Wolves start to howl in the woods.
The cities empty as we run from the epidemic.

We are footnotes; we are blinded by the flash.
We are confused and huddled in caves.
At dusk, sunsets rape the sky with colour.
They are the most beautiful we have ever seen.

2050AD

Factory

I am the things left behind,
exit wound and bi-product,
discarded catalyst, yet
still ticking with thousands
of teeth, wheels and spools.
I am cog-handed,
industrialised and ticked;
an axiom of doubt
on shifting plains.
Metalled and revolutionary;
sand to glass;
quarry to urn.
I am bi-product,
the things left behind,
the exit wound.
I move in ingraining circles.

2090AD

Quinnamon

At dawn I begin the furrow.

Ploughing mud grooves,
I do not sing as I work, few do,
but as flux of chocolate, chestnut, coffee
ripples out behind.

I think, this is better than
what we had before, when there were just buildings
and cities scraping the sky, making it ooze.

On Firstdays some of us sneak back to the city
to be *quinnamon*.
It is when you do sorry for what once was done.

Inside flows my canal.
I have been nursing it for three years now,
dredging metre by metre of syringes, prams,
broken glass, plastic, cans, cleaning the past

so we can live again.

Nothing is finished for us.
We reclaim every object, metal to blood cell,
Grandfather's body deep in the rose garden.
Bronze to knife to buckle to bell.

Yes, we still have bells, peals of them,
rolling out across miles of green,

brass mantras. The sky is a cathedral.

They denote births, deaths, marriages, *quinnamon*.
They sing the work of my hands, these furrows:

mahogany, nut, tan, terracotta. This will take me til Fifthday,
til the bells toll and I return to my canal,
deep in the twisted metropolis and do sorry,

be *quinnamon* for all those who went before.

III

Proverbs III

Pockets of memories are blue gas
in gold-mines. The struck soul is
a steel flint boot and even though
the explosions are expected,
everything's surprising in the dark.

Belief

To myself I've kept

not my creed,
but the way the creed falls.

Not the statements of faith,
but the way it feels.

You might admit that
yes, you fucked her.
But would you describe

how she felt inside
whilst you were doing it?

Perhaps only to yourself,
as she splays herself
explicitly in unexpected contexts:

at the shops, in the office,
waiting for the pasta to boil?

Same.

I wouldn't want to taint you
with too much information,

the x-rated detail,
the frantic, blind intimacy of it all.

To Caesar What is Caesar's

We flash, Neptune's silver,
a slender slick in a thick,
undulating sea.

Have I always had this tang
of mineral and metal
on the roof of my mouth,
my lipped rib-cage?

A taste of emperor's gold,
slipped disc, coin slid
by nimble fingers,
and then
a nick of hook
and a haul to the thin place,
a jerk and an up-up,
a fleeting trace of the sky above
in the place below.

And then,
mouth gaping to the coin,
silenced by the diluted air.

Ruth

Breast to breast, palms clutched and clinging,
we were gaping wombs, scrabbling for cover
as around us, the things we loved died.

Mother of corpses, she stuffs them inside,
but they rot, create cavities, collapse in on themselves.
I will burrow in her hollowness.

Slide between my dead husband, my dead brother;
pulsate, ache a promise with my widow heart that
my country will not ruin the her I have left to love.

At night I dream of an alien god kneeling
in countries beyond my control. Mara mother
grasps my hand; I will never leave her.

The dead sea is a western taunt of tears.
I rise my eyes.
A buzz and a song fills me; we walk, find lodgings.

Across borders the world still tilts.
I work a land I cannot own, but grace scratches my ankles;
Boaz moves in the fields and loves me.

The whispers of women curl my ears with their plans.
A salt-singed Rahab calls from the city wall,
Lower your basket - cover his feet with the red of your abdomen.

I fucked him on the threshing floor and longed to love again,
my fingers sore from gleaning,

my back an uncovered sunburst. He redeems my breasts.

He gleans me, picks up what is left, discovers hidden morsels,
bit by gentle bit, gathers me slowly and laboriously;
scoops me into the bloodline.

Jewish law scrolling tight in his bones.

Crucified Mann

I am a wrecked man,
planked in and sea-sored by the New Guinea moon.
I am the aquatic wound on the tyrant's shore.

At high tide the blind waves grope the black beach
and wander the cells;
zombie sullen, they reclaim a coral foot, a barnacled shin.

In her porcelain bath my woman uses a salt scrub
to chafe at her hardness.
Were it that Christ washes what the innocuous sea wets?

Now the retreating tide trails crystals on cracked feet
as the ocean drowns my soles.
Were it that Christ asks,

"Why such brutality for such a brutal man?"

World, world, why have you forsaken me?
I am sand running through his fingers.

*Simon Mann, a mercenary and old Etonian, was accused of planning
a failed coup against President Teodoro Obiang Nguema Mbasogo,
dictator of Equatorial Guinea. He is currently being held in the notorious
Blackbeach prison, which floods every time the tide comes in.*

Crucified Man

I am a splintered man,
planked in and nail-scored by the Old Jerusalem sun.
I am the blood wound on the desert's edge.

At noon the thick dark blankets the corpse
of the city I love;
apocalypse-eyed, it drowns a pierced side, a corrupted palm.

In her starkness my mother's cries violence
her throat's rawness.
Father, forgive them.

Now the dripping sponge bursts vinegar on split lips
as darkness milks my eyes.
Were it they knew

why I bear such brutality for such brutal men.

Eloi, Eloi, lama sabachthani?
I grasp the last grain.

Fortune
Venice

They say it's about painting memories,
taking photographs. Imprints of abuse.
But I have none of these. No clarity.

Just faces blurring into the carousel I ride sometimes:
London, Paris, Brighton, Venice. I bloody love those horses.
Especially the scarlet ones, burnt orange, vermillion.

Remember the worm we rode through the apple by the canal?
The gypsy ride constructed for the carnival.
The mulled wine spilled on my new salmon-pink gloves.

We were all fur and black tie. You hired a palazzo.
I danced on the balcony with the banker.
Then, later, in the four poster bed, such cold.

On the plane home we got wrecked on G&Ts.
On the carousel, my luggage burst,
you got hysterics and took photographs.

Drove me home. And now you are all army and away;
a green figure silhouetting the middle-east. Tell me this.
Will you trellis my fingers with your stories?

I want champagne and cafés,
the metal weight in your hand.
The Brideshead tenderness of your gift.

Transubstantiation

Eat This.
This is my hand, my side-skin, my right thigh;
the pouch of my cheek, the flesh of my arms.
My well-worn feet, fingernails and toes,
the skin off my teeth, the join of an arm;
sinew and bone, the gas of my stomach,
the rising of the bread.
My bile its milk.
My cuticles its crumbs.
This is my flesh, my body. Eat me.

Drink This.
This is my DNA, my iron in your wine.
My antibodies, white blood cells,
plasma, organ juice, glucose.
The string in your tooth,
the lump in your throat.
A bit of vein, artery.
Drink me before I clot.
This is my blood, my organ juice. Drink me.

Waiting for the Post

End with Amen or a clap?
I get confused.
I lose my place.
Is this a circle we're standing in?
Are we standing stones?
Is there magic here?

I think there are things in here with us.
A Jack-in-a-box, purple corners,
tumours perhaps?
An incessant buzzing.
Bruises on our knees.
And as we look we find bruises everywhere,
blue and black from front to back.

I remember when outside meant away
and I was always a stranger,
alien and wild in unfamiliar streets,
erupting from my own womb.
Can't you see my footprints
on the ocean? I've been here before.
Was it for a long time? Or a short time?
I don't know.

I don't remember much.
Reality flinches. I pull my knees up.
Balance on the surface of things.
A waxed stare. Bleached fingers.
A postcard sent from Feltham.
A broken branch on lavender seas.

A silk hat, a felt slipper.

Just things
and things I wanted.